Delicious Slow Cooker Recipes for Two

Healthy Cooking Ideas With Mouthwatering Images

by Clara Levine

Introduction

Welcome to "Delicious Slow Cooker Recipes for Two: Healthy Cooking Ideas With Mouthwatering Images," where culinary art meets simplicity. Authored by Clara Levine, this cookbook is a treasure trove for couples and companions looking to transform their mealtime into an easy, enjoyable experience.

Imagine the aroma of a slow-cooked meal greeting you at the door after a long day. This book brings you an assortment of recipes, each crafted to fit perfectly into the lives of two. Whether you're a busy duo, a health-conscious partner, or simply looking for a hassle-free cooking solution, these recipes are your answer. Every dish in this book promises a delightful taste and a nourishing experience, keeping health and well-being at its core.

Each recipe is accompanied by stunning, mouthwatering images, guiding you through the cooking process and inspiring you to try new dishes. From hearty stews and tender roasts to fresh vegetarian options and decadent desserts, you'll find an array of choices designed for the slow cooker's convenience and consistency. You'll discover that healthy cooking doesn't have to be complex or time-consuming; it can be as simple as adding ingredients to your slow cooker and letting the magic happen.

Dive into the pages of "Delicious Slow Cooker Recipes for Two" and embark on a culinary journey that's bound to enrich your cooking experience. Available in both Kindle and Paperback formats, this book is a perfect addition to your kitchen or a thoughtful gift for someone special. Embrace the ease and satisfaction of slow cooking, and let these recipes bring a new flavor to your meals. Get your copy today and enjoy healthy, delicious, and effortless cooking!

TABLE OF CONTENTS

CHAPTER 01: SEASIDE FEAST

Recipe 01: Salmon Steaks With Dill Sauce

Embark on a culinary journey with "Grilled Salmon Steaks with Dill Sauce and Salad Leaves," a delightful dish that transforms your dining experience. Crafted for couples seeking a gourmet meal with minimal fuss, this recipe combines the rich flavors of salmon with the fresh zest of dill sauce, accompanied by crisp salad leaves for a balanced meal.

Servings: 2

Prepping Time: 20 minutes

Cook Time: 2 hours on high

Difficulty: Easy

Ingredients:

- ✓ 2 salmon steaks
- ✓ 1 tablespoon olive oil
- ✓ Salt and pepper to taste
- ✓ 1/2 cup dill, finely chopped
- ✓ 1/2 cup Greek yogurt
- ✓ 1 tablespoon lemon juice
- ✓ 1 teaspoon honey
- ✓ 2 cups mixed salad leaves
- ✓ 1/2 cucumber, sliced
- ✓ 1/4 red onion, thinly sliced

Step-by-Step Preparation:

1. Brush salmon steaks with olive oil and season with salt and pepper.
2. Place salmon in the slow cooker, set it on high, and cook it for 2 hours.
3. Mix Greek yogurt, chopped dill, lemon juice, and honey in a bowl for the dill sauce. Season with salt and pepper.
4. Toss salad leaves, cucumber, and red onion in a separate bowl.
5. Once the salmon is cooked, plate it with salad on the side and drizzle with dill sauce.

Nutritional Facts: (Per serving)

- ❖ Calories: 350
- ❖ Protein: 34g
- ❖ Fat: 20g
- ❖ Carbohydrates: 8g
- ❖ Sugar: 4g
- ❖ Fiber: 2g
- ❖ Sodium: 120mg

Conclude your day on a high note with "Grilled Salmon Steaks with Dill Sauce and Salad Leaves," a dish that promises to impress with its simplicity and elegance. Perfect for a quiet evening or a special occasion, this slow-cooked masterpiece brings a taste of gourmet dining into the comfort of your home.

Recipe 02: Seer Fish Curry

Savor the flavors of the sea with "Seer Fish Curry," a dish that marries the boldness of fresh green chili with the aromatic allure of curry leaves. This slow cooker recipe is perfect for those who appreciate a meal that is both easy to prepare and rich in taste, offering a delightful twist on traditional seafood cuisine suitable for any occasion.

Servings: 2

Prepping Time: 15 minutes

Cook Time: 4 hours on low

Difficulty: Medium

Ingredients:

- ✓ 2 seer fish steaks
- ✓ 1 can coconut milk (400 ml)
- ✓ 2 tablespoons curry powder
- ✓ 1 teaspoon turmeric powder
- ✓ 1 tablespoon tamarind paste
- ✓ 1 tablespoon coconut oil
- ✓ 1 large onion, finely sliced
- ✓ 2 cloves garlic, minced
- ✓ 1 green chili, sliced
- ✓ 10 curry leaves
- ✓ Salt to taste
- ✓ 1/2 cup water

Step-by-Step Preparation:

1. Heat coconut oil, sauté onion, garlic, and green chili until softened.
2. Add curry powder and turmeric, and cook for 1 minute.
3. Transfer mixture to slow cooker; add coconut milk, tamarind paste, and water. Stir well.
4. Season fish steaks with salt and place in slow cooker.
5. Cook on low for 4 hours.
6. Garnish with fresh curry leaves and slices of green chili before serving.

Nutritional Facts: (Per serving)

- ❖ Calories: 560
- ❖ Protein: 45g
- ❖ Fat: 40g
- ❖ Carbohydrates: 15g
- ❖ Sugar: 5g
- ❖ Fiber: 3g
- ❖ Sodium: 350mg

Dive into the heartwarming comfort of "Seer Fish Curry," a dish that stands as a testament to the simplicity and beauty of slow cooking. With its tender fish steaks and a curry that is rich in flavor, this meal is an invitation to explore the depths of traditional flavors from the comfort of your home.

Recipe 03: Fish Stew Cioppino

Dive into the savory depths of "Fish Stew Cioppino with Prawns and Fish," a sumptuous seafood recipe from our Slow Cooker Cookbook. This stew celebrates the ocean's bounty, combining succulent prawns and tender fish in a rich, tomato-based broth. Perfect for seafood lovers, this dish promises a sophisticated yet comforting meal, ideal for a cozy dinner for two.

Servings: 2

Cook Time: 4 hours

Prepping Time: 20 minutes

Difficulty: Medium

Ingredients:

- ✓ 1/2 lb prawns, peeled and deveined
- ✓ 1/2 lb fish fillets, cut into chunks
- ✓ 1 can (14 oz) diced tomatoes
- ✓ 1 onion, chopped
- ✓ 2 cloves garlic, minced
- ✓ 1/2 cup fish broth
- ✓ 1/4 cup white wine
- ✓ 1 teaspoon dried basil
- ✓ 1 teaspoon dried oregano
- ✓ Salt and pepper to taste
- ✓ Fresh parsley, chopped, for garnish

Step-by-Step Preparation:

1. Place the prawns and fish in the slow cooker.
2. Add diced tomatoes, onion, garlic, fish broth, and white wine.
3. Season with basil, oregano, salt, and pepper.
4. Cook on low for 4 hours until seafood is cooked through.
5. Garnish with fresh parsley before serving.

Nutritional Facts: (Per serving)

- ❖ Calories: 300
- ❖ Protein: 40g
- ❖ Carbohydrates: 15g
- ❖ Fat: 5g
- ❖ Sodium: 700mg
- ❖ Fiber: 3g

Conclude your evening with this Fish Stew Cioppino, a dish that brings the taste of the sea straight to your table. Whether it's a special occasion or a simple night in, this recipe from our Slow Cooker Cookbook offers an easy and elegant way to enjoy a hearty, flavorful seafood stew that's sure to impress.

Recipe 04: Halibut Fish With Tomato Sauce

Savor the delicate flavors of "Baked Halibut Fish with Tomato Sauce," a refined dish from our Slow Cooker Cookbook that's sure to please any palate. This recipe features succulent halibut fillets gently baked in a savory tomato sauce, creating a perfect harmony of flavors. Ideal for a romantic dinner or a sophisticated solo meal, it's a testament to the elegance and simplicity of well-prepared seafood.

Servings: 2   **Cook Time:** 2 hours

Prepping Time: 15 minutes   **Difficulty:** Easy

Ingredients:

- ✓ 2 halibut fillets
- ✓ 1 can (14 oz) diced tomatoes
- ✓ 1 garlic clove, minced
- ✓ 1 onion, finely chopped
- ✓ 1 tablespoon olive oil
- ✓ 1 teaspoon dried basil
- ✓ Salt and pepper to taste

Step-by-Step Preparation:

1. Place the halibut fillets in the slow cooker.
2. Mix diced tomatoes, garlic, onion, olive oil, and basil in a bowl.
3. Season the mixture with salt and pepper.
4. Pour the tomato sauce over the halibut.
5. Cook on low for 2 hours until the fish is flaky and tender.
6. Serve the halibut drizzled with the cooked tomato sauce.

Nutritional Facts: (Per serving)

- ❖ Calories: 220
- ❖ Protein: 25g
- ❖ Carbohydrates: 10g
- ❖ Fat: 10g
- ❖ Sodium: 300mg
- ❖ Fiber: 2g

Conclude your dining experience with this Baked Halibut Fish with Tomato Sauce. This dish showcases the subtle yet rich flavors of the sea. Whether it's a quiet evening at home or a special occasion, this recipe from our Slow Cooker Cookbook offers a delightful way to enjoy the sophistication of halibut, enhanced by the vibrant taste of tomato sauce.

Recipe 05: Cod Fillets With Olives and Capers

Embark on a culinary journey to the Mediterranean with "Cod Fillets with Olives and Capers," a delightful dish from our Slow Cooker Cookbook. This recipe combines the light, flaky texture of cod with the salty flavors of olives and capers, creating a harmonious blend that's both refreshing and savory. Ideal for those seeking a simple yet flavorful seafood meal, it's perfect for an intimate dinner for two.

Servings: 2

Prepping Time: 15 minutes

Cook Time: 2 hours

Difficulty: Easy

Ingredients:

- ✓ 2 cod fillets
- ✓ 1/4 cup green olives, sliced
- ✓ 2 tablespoons capers
- ✓ 1 tomato, diced
- ✓ 1 garlic clove, minced
- ✓ 1 lemon, juice and zest
- ✓ 2 tablespoons olive oil
- ✓ Salt and pepper to taste
- ✓ Fresh parsley for garnish

Step-by-Step Preparation:

1. Place cod fillets in the slow cooker.
2. Top with olives, capers, and diced tomato.
3. Mix garlic, lemon juice, zest, and olive oil in a small bowl.
4. Pour the mixture over the cod.
5. Season with salt and pepper.
6. Cook on low for 2 hours until the cod is tender.
7. Garnish with fresh parsley before serving.

Nutritional Facts: (Per serving)

- ❖ Calories: 230
- ❖ Protein: 25g
- ❖ Carbohydrates: 5g
- ❖ Fat: 12g
- ❖ Sodium: 400mg
- ❖ Fiber: 1g

Conclude your meal with Cod Fillets with Olives and Capers, a dish that captures the essence of Mediterranean cuisine. Whether it's a special occasion or a weeknight dinner, this recipe from our Slow Cooker Cookbook offers a deliciously easy way to bring the flavors of the sea to your dining table, promising a satisfying and healthy meal.

Recipe 06: Grits With Cheese Shrimps Bacon

Indulge in the comforting embrace of "Grits with Cheese, Shrimps, and Bacon," a decadent recipe from our Slow Cooker Cookbook. This dish layers creamy, cheese-infused grits with succulent shrimp and crispy bacon, creating a symphony of flavors and textures. Perfect for a luxurious breakfast or a satisfying dinner, it's designed for those who appreciate a rich and flavorful meal that comforts the soul.

Servings: 2

Cook Time: 6 hours

Prepping Time: 15 minutes

Difficulty: Medium

Ingredients:

- ✓ 1/2 cup grits
- ✓ 2 cups water
- ✓ 1/2 cup cheddar cheese, grated
- ✓ 1/2 lb shrimp, peeled and deveined
- ✓ 4 slices bacon, cooked and crumbled
- ✓ Salt and pepper to taste
- ✓ 1 tablespoon butter
- ✓ Fresh parsley for garnish

Step-by-Step Preparation:

1. Combine grits and water in the slow cooker.
2. Cook on low for 6 hours until grits are soft and creamy.
3. Stir in cheddar cheese and butter until melted and smooth.
4. Season with salt and pepper.
5. Sauté shrimp until pink and cooked through.
6. Serve grits topped with shrimp and crumbled bacon.
7. Garnish with fresh parsley before serving.

Nutritional Facts: (Per serving)

- ❖ Calories: 500
- ❖ Protein: 30g
- ❖ Carbohydrates: 35g
- ❖ Fat: 25g
- ❖ Sodium: 700mg
- ❖ Fiber: 1g

Conclude your dining experience with this Grits with Cheese, shrimp, and Bacon, a dish that brings southern comfort to your table. Whether it's a leisurely weekend brunch or a cozy dinner, this recipe from our Slow Cooker Cookbook offers a delightful way to enjoy a classic dish with an indulgent twist, promising satisfaction in every bite.

Recipe 07: Prawn Paella

Embark on a culinary voyage to Spain with "Prawn Paella," a vibrant and flavorful dish from our Slow Cooker Cookbook, garnished with abundant raw vegetables, parsley, and lemon. This recipe brings the essence of traditional Spanish cuisine to your table, featuring succulent prawns amidst a bed of aromatic rice. It's perfect for those seeking a feast for the senses, combining seafood delicacy with the freshness of garden picks.

Servings: 2

Cook Time: 2.5 hours

Prepping Time: 20 minutes

Difficulty: Medium

Ingredients:

- ✓ 1 cup paella rice
- ✓ 2 cups fish stock
- ✓ 1/2 lb prawns, peeled and deveined
- ✓ 1 onion, finely chopped
- ✓ 1 bell pepper, diced
- ✓ 1 tomato, diced
- ✓ 1 garlic clove, minced
- ✓ 1 teaspoon paprika
- ✓ Salt and pepper to taste
- ✓ 1/2 lemon, for garnish
- ✓ Fresh parsley, chopped, for garnish
- ✓ A mix of raw vegetables (like cucumber and carrot sticks) for garnish

Step-by-Step Preparation:

1. Sauté onion, bell pepper, and garlic in the slow cooker on high until softened.
2. Add rice, fish stock, tomato, paprika, salt, and pepper.
3. Cook on high for 2 hours until rice is tender.
4. Add prawns and cook for an additional 30 minutes.
5. Serve the paella garnished with lemon slices, chopped parsley, and a side of raw vegetables.

Nutritional Facts: (Per serving)

- ❖ Calories: 400
- ❖ Protein: 25g
- ❖ Carbohydrates: 60g
- ❖ Fat: 5g
- ❖ Sodium: 700mg
- ❖ Fiber: 4g

Conclude your meal with this Prawn Paella, a dish that not only tantalizes your taste buds but also brings a splash of color and nutrition to your table. Whether it's a special occasion or a desire for a taste of Spain, this recipe from our Slow Cooker Cookbook offers a delightful way to enjoy a classic, bursting with the zest of lemon and the freshness of parsley.

Recipe 08: Shirmps With Asparagus

Savor the exquisite simplicity of "Shrimp with Asparagus," a refined dish from our Slow Cooker Cookbook that marries the delicate flavors of the sea with the crisp freshness of spring vegetables. This recipe is perfect for those who appreciate the elegant combination of succulent shrimp and tender asparagus cooked to perfection. It's an ideal choice for a light yet satisfying meal, showcasing the natural beauty of its ingredients.

Servings: 2

Prepping Time: 15 minutes

Cook Time: 2 hours

Difficulty: Easy

Ingredients:

- ✓ 1/2 lb shrimp, peeled and deveined
- ✓ 1 bunch asparagus, trimmed
- ✓ 2 cloves garlic, minced
- ✓ 2 tablespoons olive oil
- ✓ Salt and pepper to taste
- ✓ Lemon wedges for serving

Step-by-Step Preparation:

1. Place the shrimp and asparagus in the slow cooker.
2. Add minced garlic, drizzle with olive oil, and season with salt and pepper.
3. Toss gently to ensure an even coating.
4. Cook on low for 2 hours, until shrimp are pink and asparagus is tender.
5. Serve immediately, accompanied by lemon wedges.

Nutritional Facts: (Per serving)

- ❖ Calories: 220
- ❖ Protein: 25g
- ❖ Carbohydrates: 5g
- ❖ Fat: 12g
- ❖ Sodium: 300mg
- ❖ Fiber: 2g

Conclude your dining experience with this Shrimp with Asparagus, a dish that brings a touch of sophistication to any table. Whether it's a special occasion or a desire for a nutritious and delicious meal, this recipe from our Slow Cooker Cookbook offers a delightful way to enjoy a harmonious blend of flavors with minimal preparation and maximum satisfaction.

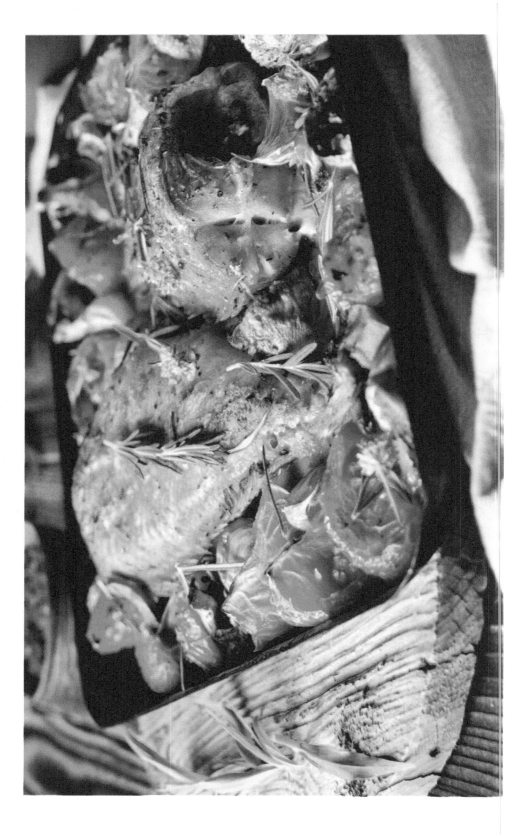

Recipe 09: Baked Sea Bass

Delve into the flavors of the ocean with "Baked Sea Bass with Tomatoes, Vegetables, and Herbs," a delectable dish from our Slow Cooker Cookbook. This recipe celebrates the delicate texture of sea bass, complemented by the robust flavors of tomatoes, a medley of fresh vegetables, and aromatic herbs. It's an ideal choice for those seeking a healthy yet flavorful seafood meal, perfect for a sophisticated dinner for two.

Servings: 2

Cook Time: 2 hours

Prepping Time: 15 minutes

Difficulty: Medium

Ingredients:

- ✓ 2 sea bass fillets
- ✓ 1 cup cherry tomatoes, halved
- ✓ 1 zucchini, sliced
- ✓ 1 bell pepper, sliced
- ✓ 1 onion, sliced
- ✓ 2 cloves garlic, minced
- ✓ 2 tablespoons olive oil
- ✓ 1 teaspoon dried thyme
- ✓ 1 teaspoon dried oregano
- ✓ Salt and pepper to taste
- ✓ Fresh parsley for garnish

Step-by-Step Preparation:

1. Place sea bass fillets in the slow cooker.
2. Surround with cherry tomatoes, zucchini, bell pepper, and onion.
3. Sprinkle minced garlic, thyme, oregano, salt, and pepper over the vegetables and fish.
4. Drizzle everything with olive oil.
5. Cook on low for 2 hours until fish is tender and vegetables are cooked.
6. Garnish with fresh parsley before serving.

Nutritional Facts: (Per serving)

- ❖ Calories: 280
- ❖ Protein: 25g
- ❖ Carbohydrates: 10g
- ❖ Fat: 16g
- ❖ Sodium: 200mg
- ❖ Fiber: 3g

Conclude your meal with this Baked Sea Bass with Tomatoes, Vegetables, and Herbs, a dish that brings a piece of the sea to your dining table. Whether it's a quiet evening at home or a special celebration, this recipe from our Slow Cooker Cookbook offers a deliciously easy way to enjoy the finesse of sea bass alongside the vibrant flavors of fresh vegetables and herbs.

Recipe 10: Lobster FRA Diavolo With Zucchini

Experience the exquisite blend of flavors with "Lobster Fra Diavolo with Zucchini, Tomatoes," a sophisticated and spicy dish from our Slow Cooker Cookbook. This culinary creation marries the luxurious taste of lobster with the fiery zest of Fra Diavolo sauce, complemented by the freshness of zucchini and tomatoes. Perfect for an intimate and memorable dining experience, it caters to those who love a dish that combines the elegance of seafood with a spicy kick.

Servings: 2

Prepping Time: 20 minutes

Cook Time: 4 hours

Difficulty: Medium

Ingredients:

- ✓ 2 lobster tails
- ✓ 1 cup marinara sauce
- ✓ 1/2 teaspoon red pepper flakes
- ✓ 1 zucchini, spiralized
- ✓ 1 cup cherry tomatoes, halved
- ✓ 1 clove garlic, minced
- ✓ 2 tablespoons olive oil
- ✓ Salt and pepper to taste
- ✓ Fresh parsley for garnish

Step-by-Step Preparation:

1. Prepare lobster tails and place them in the slow cooker.
2. Combine marinara sauce with red pepper flakes and pour over the lobster.
3. Cook on low for 4 hours until lobster is tender.
4. In a pan, sauté garlic in olive oil, add spiralized zucchini and cherry tomatoes, cooking until just tender. Season with salt and pepper.
5. Serve the lobster over the zucchini and tomato mixture, garnished with fresh parsley.

Nutritional Facts: (Per serving)

- ❖ Calories: 330
- ❖ Protein: 23g
- ❖ Carbohydrates: 12g
- ❖ Fat: 22g
- ❖ Sodium: 610mg
- ❖ Fiber: 3g

Conclude your meal with Lobster Fra Diavolo with Zucchini and tomatoes, a dish that promises a delightful journey through flavors and textures. Whether it's a special celebration or a desire for a gourmet meal at home, this recipe from our Slow Cooker Cookbook delivers an impeccable blend of luxury, spice, and freshness, making every bite an unforgettable experience.

CHAPTER 02: MEAT LOVERS' DUO

Recipe 01: Lamb's Shank With Vegatables

Immerse yourself in the rich and tender flavors of "Lamb Shank with Vegetables," a sumptuous dish from our Slow Cooker Cookbook. This recipe perfectly slow-cooks the lamb shanks until they fall-off-the-bone tender, accompanied by a hearty blend of vegetables.

Servings: 2   **Cook Time:** 8 hours

Prepping Time: 20 minutes   **Difficulty:** Medium

Ingredients:

- ✓ 2 lamb shanks
- ✓ 2 carrots, chopped
- ✓ 2 potatoes, cubed
- ✓ 1 onion, sliced
- ✓ 2 cloves garlic, minced

- ✓ 2 cups beef broth
- ✓ 1 teaspoon rosemary
- ✓ 1 teaspoon thyme
- ✓ Salt and pepper to taste
- ✓ Olive oil

Step-by-Step Preparation:

1. Season lamb shanks with salt, pepper, rosemary, and thyme.
2. In a skillet, heat olive oil and brown the lamb shanks on all sides.
3. Place the lamb shanks in the slow cooker.
4. Add the chopped vegetables around the lamb.
5. Pour beef broth over the ingredients.
6. Cook on low for 8 hours until the lamb is tender.
7. Serve the lamb shanks with the vegetables, spooning over the juices as sauce.

Nutritional Facts: (Per serving)

- ❖ Calories: 500
- ❖ Protein: 60g
- ❖ Carbohydrates: 40g

- ❖ Fat: 15g
- ❖ Sodium: 700mg
- ❖ Fiber: 5g

Conclude your meal with Lamb Shank with Vegetables, a dish that brings the comfort and warmth of slow cooking to your table. Whether it's a special occasion or a cozy night in, this recipe from our Slow Cooker Cookbook offers a delightful way to enjoy the robust flavors of lamb, tenderly paired with the earthiness of seasonal vegetables, for a truly satisfying dining experience.

Recipe 02: Beef Bourguignon

Embark on a culinary journey to the heart of France with "Beef Bourguignon Stew," a luxurious recipe from our Slow Cooker Cookbook. This dish is a symphony of flavors, featuring tender beef marinated in red wine and cooked with carrots, onions, and garlic, infused with a bouquet of garni. The stew is elegantly garnished with pearl onions, mushrooms, and crispy bacon, offering a taste of French sophistication right at your table.

Servings: 2   **Cook Time:** 8 hours

Prepping Time: 30 minutes   **Difficulty:** Medium

Ingredients:

- ✓ 1 lb beef chuck, cut into cubes
- ✓ 1 cup red wine
- ✓ 2 carrots, sliced
- ✓ 1 large onion, chopped
- ✓ 2 cloves garlic, minced
- ✓ 1 bouquet garni (thyme, bay leaf, and parsley)
- ✓ 1/2 cup pearl onions
- ✓ 1/2 cup mushrooms, sliced
- ✓ 4 slices bacon, chopped
- ✓ Salt and pepper to taste
- ✓ 2 tablespoons flour
- ✓ 2 tablespoons olive oil

Step-by-Step Preparation:

1. Season beef with salt and pepper, then dust with flour.
2. Brown the meat in olive oil in a skillet, then transfer to the slow cooker.
3. In the same skillet, cook bacon until crisp; add to the slow cooker.
4. Sauté onions, carrots, and garlic in the skillet; add to the slow cooker with the bouquet garni.
5. Pour red wine into the slow cooker, covering the ingredients.
6. Cook on low for 8 hours until beef is tender.
7. In the last hour, add pearl onions and mushrooms.
8. Serve the stew garnished with additional fresh herbs.

Nutritional Facts: (Per serving)

- ❖ Calories: 600
- ❖ Protein: 40g
- ❖ Carbohydrates: 20g
- ❖ Fat: 35g
- ❖ Sodium: 500mg
- ❖ Fiber: 3g

Conclude your meal with Beef Bourguignon Stew, a dish that encapsulates the warmth and richness of French cuisine. Whether it's a cozy dinner for two or a special occasion, this recipe from our Slow Cooker Cookbook offers a delightful way to savor the complex layers of flavors and textures, making every bite a luxurious experience.

Recipe 03: Beef Osso Buco

Indulge in the hearty and luxurious "Osso buco Meat Stew on the Bone," a masterpiece recipe from our Slow Cooker Cookbook. This traditional Italian dish features tender veal shanks, slow-cooked to perfection in a rich vegetable sauce with carrots, tomatoes, and celery. It's a celebration of flavors and textures, perfect for those who appreciate the depth and richness of slow-cooked meat and garden vegetables' freshness.

Servings: 2   **Cook Time:** 8 hours

Prepping Time: 25 minutes   **Difficulty:** Medium

Ingredients:

- ✓ 2 veal shanks
- ✓ 1 cup diced carrots
- ✓ 1 cup diced tomatoes
- ✓ 1 cup diced celery
- ✓ 1 onion, chopped
- ✓ 2 cloves garlic, minced
- ✓ 2 cups beef broth
- ✓ 1 teaspoon dried thyme
- ✓ Salt and pepper to taste
- ✓ 2 tablespoons olive oil
- ✓ Fresh parsley for garnish

Step-by-Step Preparation:

1. Season veal shanks with salt and pepper.
2. In a skillet, heat olive oil and brown the shanks on both sides.
3. Transfer the shanks to the slow cooker.
4. In the same skillet, sauté onion, carrots, celery, and garlic until softened.
5. Add the vegetables to the slow cooker with the veal.
6. Pour in beef broth and sprinkle with thyme.
7. Cook on low for 8 hours until the meat is fall-off-the-bone tender.
8. Garnish with fresh parsley before serving.

Nutritional Facts: (Per serving)

- ❖ Calories: 600
- ❖ Protein: 50g
- ❖ Carbohydrates: 20g
- ❖ Fat: 35g
- ❖ Sodium: 700mg
- ❖ Fiber: 5g

Conclude your dining experience with Ossobuco Meat Stew on the Bone. This dish offers a sumptuous taste of Italian culinary tradition. Perfect for a special dinner or a comforting weekend meal, this recipe from our Slow Cooker Cookbook brings the rich, slow-cooked flavors of osso buco to your home, making every bite a celebration of gourmet craftsmanship and home-cooked warmth.

Recipe 04: Duck a L'Orange Fillet

Embrace the elegance of French cuisine with "Duck à l'Orange," a refined dish featured in our Slow Cooker Cookbook. This classic recipe pairs the rich flavor of duck fillets with a vibrant orange sauce, beautifully garnished with fresh orange slices and redcurrant berries. It's designed for those who appreciate the delicate balance of savory duck with citrus's sweet and tangy notes, offering a luxurious dining experience.

Servings: 2

Prepping Time: 20 minutes

Cook Time: 4 hours

Difficulty: Medium

Ingredients:

- ✓ 2 duck breast fillets
- ✓ 1 cup orange juice
- ✓ 1 tablespoon orange zest
- ✓ 2 tablespoons honey
- ✓ 1 tablespoon balsamic vinegar
- ✓ Salt and pepper to taste
- ✓ Fresh orange slices for garnish
- ✓ Redcurrant berries for garnish

Step-by-Step Preparation:

1. Season duck breasts with salt and pepper.
2. Place in the slow cooker.
3. Mix orange juice, zest, honey, and vinegar in a bowl. Pour over the duck.
4. Cook on low for 4 hours until the duck is tender.
5. Serve fillets with the orange sauce, garnished with orange slices and redcurrant berries.

Nutritional Facts: (Per serving)

- ❖ Calories: 420
- ❖ Protein: 30g
- ❖ Carbohydrates: 25g
- ❖ Fat: 20g
- ❖ Sodium: 200mg
- ❖ Fiber: 1g

Conclude your meal with Duck à l'Orange, a dish that promises an unforgettable journey through the sophistication of French cooking. Whether it's a celebration or a desire for a gourmet meal at home, this recipe from our Slow Cooker Cookbook delivers a feast for the senses, combining the richness of duck with the freshness of orange for a truly exquisite experience.

Recipe 05: Beef and Broccoli

Dive into the savory delight of "Thinly Sliced Beef and Broccoli in a Savory Sauce," a mouthwatering dish from our Slow Cooker Cookbook. This recipe pairs tender slices of beef with crisp, fresh broccoli, all coated in a rich and flavorful sauce. It's perfect for those seeking a delicious, hearty meal that combines the robust taste of beef with the healthful broccoli crunch, making it an ideal dinner for two.

Servings: 2

Cook Time: 6 hours

Prepping Time: 15 minutes

Difficulty: Easy

Ingredients:

- ✓ 1/2 lb beef, thinly sliced
- ✓ 2 cups broccoli florets
- ✓ 1 onion, sliced
- ✓ 2 cloves garlic, minced
- ✓ 1/2 cup beef broth
- ✓ 1/4 cup soy sauce
- ✓ 2 tablespoons brown sugar
- ✓ 1 tablespoon sesame oil
- ✓ 1 teaspoon cornstarch
- ✓ Salt and pepper to taste

Step-by-Step Preparation:

1. Place the beef and broccoli in the slow cooker.
2. Mix beef broth, soy sauce, brown sugar, sesame oil, and garlic in a bowl.
3. Pour the sauce over the beef and broccoli.
4. Cook on low for 6 hours until the meat is tender.
5. Mix cornstarch with water and stir into the cooker to thicken the sauce.
6. Serve hot, seasoned with salt and pepper to taste.

Nutritional Facts: (Per serving)

- ❖ Calories: 300
- ❖ Protein: 25g
- ❖ Carbohydrates: 20g
- ❖ Fat: 15g
- ❖ Sodium: 1100mg
- ❖ Fiber: 3g

Conclude your dining experience with Thinly Sliced Beef and Broccoli in a Savory Sauce. This dish effortlessly combines beef's rich flavors with broccoli's vibrant freshness. Whether it's a weeknight dinner or a special occasion, this recipe from our Slow Cooker Cookbook offers a satisfying and flavorful way to enjoy a balanced and delicious meal.

Recipe 06: Lamb Meat Curry

Embark on a flavorful journey with "Lamb Meat with Curry Sauce," a standout dish from our Slow Cooker Cookbook. This recipe expertly combines tender lamb with a rich, aromatic curry sauce, offering a symphony of spices that tantalize the taste buds. Perfect for those who crave the deep, complex flavors of curry paired with succulent meat, it's an ideal meal for a cozy dinner for two.

Servings: 2

Cook Time: 8 hours

Prepping Time: 20 minutes

Difficulty: Medium

Ingredients:

- ✓ 1 lb lamb, cut into chunks
- ✓ 1 onion, chopped
- ✓ 2 cloves garlic, minced
- ✓ 1 tablespoon curry powder
- ✓ 1 teaspoon turmeric
- ✓ 1 can (14 oz) coconut milk
- ✓ 1/2 cup chicken broth
- ✓ Salt and pepper to taste
- ✓ Fresh cilantro for garnish

Step-by-Step Preparation:

1. Season lamb with salt and pepper.
2. Place lamb, onion, and garlic in the slow cooker.
3. Sprinkle with curry powder and turmeric.
4. Pour coconut milk and chicken broth over the meat.
5. Cook on low for 8 hours until lamb is tender.
6. Serve garnished with fresh cilantro.

Nutritional Facts: (Per serving)

- ❖ Calories: 580
- ❖ Protein: 40g
- ❖ Carbohydrates: 15g
- ❖ Fat: 40g
- ❖ Sodium: 300mg
- ❖ Fiber: 2g

Conclude your meal with Lamb Meat with Curry Sauce, a dish that promises a culinary adventure with every bite. Whether it's a special occasion or a desire for a flavorful escape, this recipe from our Slow Cooker Cookbook delivers an unforgettable dining experience, showcasing the perfect blend of tender lamb and aromatic spices.

Recipe 07: Braised Beef and Mushrooms

Savor the rich and comforting flavors of "Braised Beef and Mushrooms," a heartwarming dish from our Slow Cooker Cookbook. This recipe combines succulent beef and earthy mushrooms in a savory sauce, slow-cooked to perfection. Ideal for those seeking an intensely flavorful and tender meal, it's a perfect choice for a cozy dinner for two, embodying the essence of home-cooked comfort and sophistication.

Servings: 2

Prepping Time: 20 minutes

Cook Time: 8 hours

Difficulty: Easy

Ingredients:

- ✓ 1 lb beef chuck, cut into chunks
- ✓ 1 cup mushrooms, sliced
- ✓ 1 onion, chopped
- ✓ 2 cloves garlic, minced
- ✓ 1 cup beef broth
- ✓ 2 tablespoons tomato paste
- ✓ 1 teaspoon thyme
- ✓ Salt and pepper to taste
- ✓ 2 tablespoons olive oil

Step-by-Step Preparation:

1. Season beef with salt and pepper.
2. In a skillet, heat olive oil and brown the beef on all sides. Transfer to the slow cooker.
3. In the same skillet, sauté onions, garlic, and mushrooms. Add to the slow cooker.
4. Stir in beef broth, tomato paste, and thyme.
5. Cook on low for 8 hours until beef is tender.
6. Serve the braised beef and mushrooms with the rich sauce.

Nutritional Facts: (Per serving)

- ❖ Calories: 450
- ❖ Protein: 35g
- ❖ Carbohydrates: 10g
- ❖ Fat: 30g
- ❖ Sodium: 300mg
- ❖ Fiber: 2g

Conclude your meal with Braised Beef and Mushrooms, a dish that marries simplicity with rich, umami flavors. Whether it's a special night or you're simply craving a comforting meal, this recipe from our Slow Cooker Cookbook offers a delicious way to enjoy classic ingredients, transforming them into a tender, flavorful feast that's sure to impress.

Recipe 08: Spicy Lamb Chops

Indulge in the exotic flavors of "Spicy Lamb Chops with Couscous and Vegetables," a culinary masterpiece from our Slow Cooker Cookbook. This dish features succulent lamb chops, perfectly paired with fluffy couscous and a medley of vegetables, all brought together with a unique sauce of caramel, pepper, and spices. It's a feast for the senses, ideal for those seeking a gourmet meal that combines rich flavors and tender textures.

Servings: 2

Cook Time: 6 hours

Prepping Time: 20 minutes

Difficulty: Medium

Ingredients:

- ✓ 2 lamb chops
- ✓ 1 cup couscous
- ✓ 1 cup mixed vegetables (carrots, zucchini, bell peppers)
- ✓ 1/2 cup beef broth
- ✓ 2 tablespoons caramel sauce
- ✓ 1 teaspoon ground black pepper
- ✓ 1 teaspoon mixed dried spices (cumin, coriander, cinnamon)
- ✓ Salt to taste
- ✓ Olive oil

Step-by-Step Preparation:

1. Season lamb chops with salt, pepper, and spices.
2. In the slow cooker, place the lamb chops and drizzle with olive oil.
3. Add mixed vegetables around the chops.
4. Pour beef broth over the ingredients.
5. Cook on low for 6 hours until lamb is tender.
6. Prepare couscous according to package instructions.
7. Serve lamb chops over couscous, topped with vegetables, and drizzled with caramel sauce.

Nutritional Facts: (Per serving)

- ❖ Calories: 550
- ❖ Protein: 35g
- ❖ Carbohydrates: 60g
- ❖ Fat: 20g
- ❖ Sodium: 300mg
- ❖ Fiber: 5g

Conclude your dining experience with Lamb Chops with Couscous and Vegetables, a dish that satisfies your hunger and transports you to a world of complex flavors and aromas. Whether it's a special occasion or a lavish dinner for two, this recipe from our Slow Cooker Cookbook offers a delightful way to enjoy the richness of lamb combined with the sweetness of caramel and the warmth of spices.

Recipe 09: Beef Stroganoff With Pasta

Embark on a culinary journey with "Beef Stroganoff with Pasta," a classic dish reimagined in our Slow Cooker Cookbook. This comforting meal combines tender beef strips in a rich, creamy sauce, served over a bed of perfectly cooked pasta. It's an ideal choice for those seeking a hearty and satisfying dish that marries the robust flavors of beef with the creamy texture of stroganoff sauce.

Servings: 2

Cook Time: 8 hours

Prepping Time: 20 minutes

Difficulty: Easy

Ingredients:

- ✓ 1/2 lb beef sirloin, thinly sliced
- ✓ 1 cup mushrooms, sliced
- ✓ 1 onion, finely chopped
- ✓ 1 clove garlic, minced
- ✓ 1 cup beef broth
- ✓ 1/2 cup sour cream
- ✓ 2 tablespoons all-purpose flour
- ✓ 1 tablespoon Worcestershire sauce
- ✓ Salt and pepper to taste
- ✓ 2 cups cooked pasta

Step-by-Step Preparation:

1. Place beef, mushrooms, onion, and garlic in the slow cooker.
2. Whisk together beef broth, flour, Worcestershire sauce, salt, and pepper in a bowl. Pour over the beef mixture.
3. Cook on low for 8 hours until beef is tender.
4. Stir in sour cream during the last 30 minutes of cooking.
5. Serve the beef stroganoff over cooked pasta.

Nutritional Facts: (Per serving)

- ❖ Calories: 650
- ❖ Protein: 40g
- ❖ Carbohydrates: 60g
- ❖ Fat: 25g
- ❖ Sodium: 700mg
- ❖ Fiber: 3g

Conclude your meal with Beef Stroganoff with Pasta, a dish that offers a comforting embrace with every bite. Whether it's a chilly evening or a special dinner, this recipe from our Slow Cooker Cookbook delivers a deliciously rich and creamy experience, making it a timeless favorite for a cozy night in.

Recipe 10: Pulled Beef Brisket

Immerse yourself in the deep, savory flavors of "Pulled Beef Brisket," a standout dish from our Slow Cooker Cookbook. This recipe meticulously slow-cooks the beef brisket until it's irresistibly tender and easily shredded, infused with a blend of spices that enhance its natural flavors. It's perfect for those who appreciate the art of slow cooking, yielding a mouthwatering meal that's both satisfying and versatile.

Servings: 2

Cook Time: 10 hours

Prepping Time: 20 minutes

Difficulty: Easy

Ingredients:

- ✓ 1 lb beef brisket
- ✓ 1 cup beef broth
- ✓ 2 tablespoons brown sugar
- ✓ 1 tablespoon paprika
- ✓ 1 teaspoon garlic powder
- ✓ 1 teaspoon onion powder
- ✓ Salt and pepper to taste
- ✓ Barbecue sauce for serving

Step-by-Step Preparation:

1. Mix brown sugar, paprika, garlic powder, onion powder, salt, and pepper. Rub this mixture all over the brisket.
2. Place the seasoned brisket in the slow cooker.
3. Pour beef broth around the brisket.
4. Cook on low for 10 hours until the brisket is very tender.
5. Shred the meat with two forks.
6. Serve the pulled beef brisket with barbecue sauce.

Nutritional Facts: (Per serving)

- ❖ Calories: 600
- ❖ Protein: 60g
- ❖ Carbohydrates: 20g
- ❖ Fat: 30g
- ❖ Sodium: 700mg
- ❖ Fiber: 1g

Conclude your meal with Pulled Beef Brisket, a dish that promises a flavorful journey with every bite. Whether served in a sandwich, alongside your favorite sides or as the star of your dinner plate, this recipe from our Slow Cooker Cookbook delivers a tender, flavorful brisket that's sure to impress, making it a cherished meal for any occasion.

CHAPTER 03: CHICKEN CUDDLES

Recipe 01: Chicken With Rosemary

Delight in the rustic and aromatic flavors of "Chicken in Tomato Sauce with Rosemary and Thyme," a heartwarming recipe from our Slow Cooker Cookbook. This dish bathes tender chicken in a rich tomato sauce, fragrantly seasoned with rosemary and thyme, offering a perfect blend of herbs and spices. It's an ideal meal for those seeking comfort food with a sophisticated twist, making any dinner memorable.

Servings: 2

Prepping Time: 15 minutes

Cook Time: 6 hours

Difficulty: Easy

Ingredients:

- ✓ 2 chicken drumsticks
- ✓ 1 can (14 oz) diced tomatoes
- ✓ 1 onion, chopped
- ✓ 2 cloves garlic, minced
- ✓ 1 teaspoon fresh rosemary, chopped
- ✓ 1 teaspoon fresh thyme, chopped
- ✓ Salt and pepper to taste
- ✓ 2 tablespoons olive oil

Step-by-Step Preparation:

1. Season chicken drumsticks with salt and pepper.
2. Combine diced tomatoes, onion, garlic, rosemary, and thyme in the slow cooker.
3. Place the seasoned chicken in the tomato mixture.
4. Drizzle olive oil over the chicken.
5. Cook on low for 6 hours, until the chicken is tender and the sauce is flavorful.
6. Serve the chicken smothered in the herb-infused tomato sauce.

Nutritional Facts: (Per serving)

- ❖ Calories: 300
- ❖ Protein: 35g
- ❖ Carbohydrates: 10g
- ❖ Fat: 14g
- ❖ Sodium: 300mg
- ❖ Fiber: 2g

Conclude your meal with Chicken in Tomato Sauce with Rosemary and Thyme. This dish combines the simplicity of slow cooking with the depth of Mediterranean flavors. Whether it's a quiet evening at home or a gathering with loved ones, this recipe from our Slow Cooker Cookbook offers a delicious and easy way to enjoy a flavorful, herbaceous chicken dish that's sure to comfort and satisfy.

Recipe 02: Chicken Cacciatore

Embark on a flavorful journey with "Chicken Cacciatore," a classic Italian dish reimagined in our Slow Cooker Cookbook. This recipe combines tender chicken breasts with a vibrant mix of tomatoes, bell peppers, carrots, and sliced mushrooms, all simmered to perfection. It's designed for those who cherish hearty, comforting meals that bring a touch of Italian countryside to the dinner table, making any meal feel like a special occasion.

Servings: 2

Cook Time: 8 hours

Prepping Time: 20 minutes

Difficulty: Easy

Ingredients:

- ✓ 2 chicken breasts
- ✓ 1 can (14 oz) diced tomatoes
- ✓ 1 bell pepper, sliced
- ✓ 2 carrots, sliced
- ✓ 1 cup sliced mushrooms

- ✓ 1 onion, chopped
- ✓ 2 cloves garlic, minced
- ✓ 1 teaspoon dried oregano
- ✓ Salt and pepper to taste
- ✓ 2 tablespoons olive oil

Step-by-Step Preparation:

1. Season chicken breasts with salt and pepper.
2. Layer the onions, bell pepper, carrots, and mushrooms in the slow cooker.
3. Place the seasoned chicken on top of the vegetables.
4. Pour diced tomatoes over the chicken and sprinkle with garlic and oregano.
5. Drizzle everything with olive oil.
6. Cook on low for 8 hours, until the chicken is tender and the vegetables are soft.
7. Serve the chicken cacciatore hot, enjoying the melding of flavors.

Nutritional Facts: (Per serving)

- ❖ Calories: 350
- ❖ Protein: 30g
- ❖ Carbohydrates: 20g

- ❖ Fat: 16g
- ❖ Sodium: 400mg
- ❖ Fiber: 4g

Conclude your dining experience with Chicken Cacciatore, a dish that promises a heartwarming blend of flavors and textures. Whether it's a weeknight dinner or a leisurely weekend meal, this recipe from our Slow Cooker Cookbook delivers a delicious and nourishing way to enjoy the simplicity and richness of Italian cooking right in your home.

Recipe 03: Chicken Marsala

Dive into the exquisite flavors of "Chicken Marsala," a celebrated dish from our Slow Cooker Cookbook that combines tender chicken cutlets with earthy mushrooms and the deep, aromatic Marsala wine. Enhanced with a garnish of perfectly cooked potatoes, this dish offers a gourmet dining experience. Ideal for those who relish the fusion of succulent poultry and robust flavors, it transforms an everyday meal into a memorable feast.

Servings: 2

Cook Time: 5 hours

Prepping Time: 20 minutes

Difficulty: Easy

Ingredients:

- ✓ 2 chicken cutlets
- ✓ 1 cup sliced mushrooms
- ✓ 1/2 cup Marsala wine
- ✓ 1 cup chicken broth
- ✓ 2 tablespoons all-purpose flour
- ✓ 2 tablespoons butter
- ✓ Salt and pepper to taste
- ✓ 2 potatoes, cooked and sliced for garnish

Step-by-Step Preparation:

1. Season chicken cutlets with salt and pepper, then dust with flour.
2. In the slow cooker, melt butter and add the chicken.
3. Top with sliced mushrooms.
4. Pour Marsala wine and chicken broth over the chicken and mushrooms.
5. Cook on low for 5 hours until the chicken is tender.
6. Serve the chicken and mushrooms with the sauce, garnished with sliced potatoes.

Nutritional Facts: (Per serving)

- ❖ Calories: 450
- ❖ Protein: 30g
- ❖ Carbohydrates: 35g
- ❖ Fat: 20g
- ❖ Sodium: 300mg
- ❖ Fiber: 4g

Conclude your meal with Chicken Marsala, a dish that elegantly showcases the richness of Marsala wine melded with the tenderness of chicken and the rustic flavor of mushrooms. Whether it's a special dinner or a desire for a comforting, sophisticated meal, this recipe from our Slow Cooker Cookbook delivers a satisfying and flavorful experience, beautifully accented by the hearty garnish of potatoes.

Recipe 04: Chicken Alfredo

Embark on a creamy culinary adventure with "Chicken Alfredo Pasta with Chicken Pieces and Broccoli," a sumptuous creation from our Slow Cooker Cookbook. This dish marries the juiciness of chicken pieces with the freshness of broccoli; all enveloped in a velvety Alfredo sauce and tender pasta. It's designed for those who cherish the comfort of pasta dishes infused with Alfredo's richness and broccoli's nutritional goodness.

Servings: 2

Prepping Time: 15 minutes

Cook Time: 4 hours

Difficulty: Easy

Ingredients:

- ✓ 2 chicken breasts, cut into pieces
- ✓ 1 cup broccoli florets
- ✓ 1 cup Alfredo sauce
- ✓ 1/2 pound pasta, cooked
- ✓ Salt and pepper to taste
- ✓ 1/2 cup grated Parmesan cheese

Step-by-Step Preparation:

1. Season chicken pieces with salt and pepper and place in the slow cooker.
2. Add broccoli and Alfredo sauce over the chicken.
3. Cook on low for 4 hours until chicken is tender.
4. Combine the chicken and broccoli mixture with cooked pasta.
5. Serve garnished with grated Parmesan cheese.

Nutritional Facts: (Per serving)

- ❖ Calories: 650
- ❖ Protein: 50g
- ❖ Carbohydrates: 50g
- ❖ Fat: 25g
- ❖ Sodium: 900mg
- ❖ Fiber: 3g

Conclude your meal with Chicken Alfredo Pasta with Chicken Pieces and Broccoli, a dish that encapsulates the essence of indulgent dining while incorporating the wholesomeness of broccoli. Whether it's a special occasion or a need for a comforting meal, this recipe from our Slow Cooker Cookbook offers a perfect blend of taste, texture, and nutrition, making it a delightful choice for any pasta lover.

Recipe 05: Chicken Tikka Masala

Embark on a flavorful journey with "Chicken Tikka Masala," a beloved dish from our Slow Cooker Cookbook that brings the vibrant tastes of India to your kitchen. This recipe combines tender chicken marinated in a rich, spiced sauce, offering a perfect balance of warmth and creaminess. Ideal for those seeking to indulge in the complexity of Indian cuisine, it's a comforting meal that promises to delight and satisfy.

Servings: 2

Cook Time: 6 hours

Prepping Time: 20 minutes

Difficulty: Medium

Ingredients:

- ✓ 2 chicken breasts, cut into chunks
- ✓ 1 cup yogurt
- ✓ 1 can (14 oz) tomato sauce
- ✓ 1 onion, finely chopped
- ✓ 2 cloves garlic, minced
- ✓ 2 tablespoons Tikka Masala spice blend
- ✓ 1 teaspoon ginger, grated
- ✓ Salt to taste
- ✓ 1/4 cup heavy cream
- ✓ Fresh cilantro for garnish

Step-by-Step Preparation:

1. Marinate chicken in yogurt and Tikka Masala spice blend for 1 hour.
2. Place chicken, onion, garlic, ginger, and tomato sauce in the slow cooker.
3. Season with salt.
4. Cook on low for 6 hours until chicken is tender.
5. Stir in heavy cream just before serving.
6. Garnish with fresh cilantro.

Nutritional Facts: (Per serving)

- ❖ Calories: 450
- ❖ Protein: 35g
- ❖ Carbohydrates: 20g
- ❖ Fat: 25g
- ❖ Sodium: 800mg
- ❖ Fiber: 3g

Conclude your dining experience with Chicken Tikka Masala, a dish with a harmonious blend of spices, creaminess, and juiciness. Whether you're a connoisseur of Indian cuisine or exploring new flavors, this recipe from our Slow Cooker Cookbook provides a simple yet authentic way to enjoy a classic dish that's both nourishing and full of flavor.

Recipe 06: Lemon Garlic Chicken

Savor the classic flavors of "Grilled Chicken with Butter, Lemon, and Garlic," a delectable dish from our Slow Cooker Cookbook. This recipe elevates the simple grilled chicken with rich butter, zesty lemon, and aromatic garlic. Perfect for those seeking a meal that's both comforting and bursting with flavor, it's an ideal choice for a cozy dinner for two.

Servings: 2

Prepping Time: 15 minutes

Cook Time: 4 hours

Difficulty: Easy

Ingredients:

- ✓ 2 chicken breasts
- ✓ 4 tablespoons butter
- ✓ 1 lemon, juiced and zested
- ✓ 2 cloves garlic, minced
- ✓ Salt and pepper to taste
- ✓ Fresh parsley for garnish

Step-by-Step Preparation:

1. Season chicken breasts with salt and pepper.
2. Place in the slow cooker.
3. Mix butter, lemon juice, zest, and garlic in a small bowl.
4. Pour the butter mixture over the chicken.
5. Cook on low for 4 hours until chicken is tender.
6. Garnish with fresh parsley before serving.

Nutritional Facts: (Per serving)

- ❖ Calories: 400
- ❖ Protein: 25g
- ❖ Carbohydrates: 3g
- ❖ Fat: 32g
- ❖ Sodium: 220mg
- ❖ Fiber: 0.5g

Conclude your meal with Grilled Chicken with Butter, Lemon, and Garlic. This dish combines the simplicity of grilled chicken with the elegance of buttery lemon garlic sauce. Whether dining al fresco or enjoying a quiet night in, this recipe from our Slow Cooker Cookbook offers a delicious way to enjoy a classic combination of flavors that's sure to impress.

Recipe 07: Chicken Parmigiana

Indulge in the comforting flavors of "Chicken Parmigiana with Linguini Pasta, Cheese, and Sauce," a classic dish from our Slow Cooker Cookbook that brings the taste of Italy into your home. This recipe combines the juiciness of chicken parmigiana, smothered in a rich tomato sauce and melted cheese, with the al dente perfection of linguini pasta. It's designed for those who love a hearty, flavorful meal that marries the juiciness of chicken with the indulgence of Italian pasta and cheeses.

Servings: 2

Prepping Time: 20 minutes

Cook Time: 4 hours

Difficulty: Medium

Ingredients:

- ✓ 2 chicken breasts
- ✓ 1 cup breadcrumbs
- ✓ 1/2 cup grated Parmesan cheese, plus extra for serving
- ✓ 1 cup marinara sauce
- ✓ 1/2 cup shredded mozzarella cheese
- ✓ 1/2 pound linguini pasta, cooked
- ✓ Salt and pepper to taste
- ✓ 1 egg, beaten
- ✓ 2 tablespoons olive oil

Step-by-Step Preparation:

1. Season chicken breasts with salt and pepper, dip in beaten egg, then coat in a mixture of breadcrumbs and grated Parmesan.
2. In a skillet, heat olive oil and brown the chicken on both sides.
3. Place browned chicken in the slow cooker and top with marinara sauce.
4. Cook on low for 4 hours until chicken is tender.
5. Sprinkle mozzarella cheese over chicken in the last 30 minutes of cooking.
6. Serve the chicken over linguini pasta, garnished with extra Parmesan cheese.

Nutritional Facts: (Per serving)

- ❖ Calories: 670
- ❖ Protein: 58g
- ❖ Carbohydrates: 78g
- ❖ Fat: 22g
- ❖ Sodium: 950mg
- ❖ Fiber: 5g

Conclude your meal with Chicken Parmigiana with Linguini Pasta, Cheese, and Sauce. This dish promises a delightful exploration of textures and tastes. Whether it's a cozy dinner for two or a celebration of Italian cuisine, this recipe from our Slow Cooker Cookbook delivers a rich and satisfying experience that will surely be cherished by all who partake.

Recipe 08: Chicken Fajitas

Embark on a culinary adventure with "Chicken Fajitas with Vegetables," a vibrant and flavorful dish from our Slow Cooker Cookbook. This recipe marries tender chicken with a colorful array of bell peppers and onions infused with Mexican spices. It's perfect for those seeking a festive and easy-to-prepare meal that's both nutritious and packed with flavor, bringing the essence of Tex-Mex cuisine to your table.

Servings: 2

Prepping Time: 15 minutes

Cook Time: 4 hours

Difficulty: Easy

Ingredients:

- ✓ 2 chicken breasts, sliced
- ✓ 1 red bell pepper, sliced
- ✓ 1 green bell pepper, sliced
- ✓ 1 onion, sliced
- ✓ 2 cloves garlic, minced
- ✓ 1 tablespoon taco seasoning
- ✓ Salt and pepper to taste
- ✓ Tortillas, for serving

Step-by-Step Preparation:

1. Place sliced chicken, bell peppers, onion, and garlic in the slow cooker.
2. Sprinkle with taco seasoning, salt, and pepper.
3. Cook on low for 4 hours until chicken is tender and vegetables are soft.
4. Serve the chicken and vegetables with warm tortillas.

Nutritional Facts: (Per serving)

- ❖ Calories: 300
- ❖ Protein: 26g
- ❖ Carbohydrates: 20g
- ❖ Fat: 12g
- ❖ Sodium: 500mg
- ❖ Fiber: 3g

Conclude your meal with Chicken Fajitas with Vegetables, a dish that encapsulates the joy of sharing good food. Whether it's a weeknight dinner or a special occasion, this recipe from our Slow Cooker Cookbook offers a delightful way to enjoy the simplicity of fajitas, transforming everyday ingredients into a feast for the senses.

Recipe 09: Chicken Liver Stroganoff

Delve into the rich and creamy world of "Stroganoff Chicken Liver with Mushrooms and Cream," a luxurious dish from our Slow Cooker Cookbook. This recipe transforms chicken liver into a delicacy, combined with earthy mushrooms and enveloped in a velvety cream sauce. Perfect for those who appreciate the depth of flavor that chicken liver offers, this dish is a comforting, gourmet experience designed to satisfy sophisticated palates.

Servings: 2

Cook Time: 4 hours

Prepping Time: 15 minutes

Difficulty: Medium

Ingredients:

- ✓ 1/2 lb chicken liver, cleaned and trimmed
- ✓ 1 cup mushrooms, sliced
- ✓ 1 onion, chopped
- ✓ 1 clove garlic, minced
- ✓ 1 cup heavy cream
- ✓ 1/2 cup beef broth
- ✓ 2 tablespoons all-purpose flour
- ✓ 1 teaspoon paprika
- ✓ Salt and pepper to taste
- ✓ Fresh parsley, chopped, for garnish

Step-by-Step Preparation:

1. Season chicken liver with salt, pepper, and paprika.
2. Dredge the liver in flour.
3. Combine chicken liver, mushrooms, onion, and garlic in the slow cooker.
4. Pour in beef broth and cook on low for 4 hours.
5. Stir in heavy cream during the last 30 minutes of cooking.
6. Serve garnished with fresh parsley.

Nutritional Facts: (Per serving)

- ❖ Calories: 500
- ❖ Protein: 25g
- ❖ Carbohydrates: 15g
- ❖ Fat: 40g
- ❖ Sodium: 300mg
- ❖ Fiber: 2g

Conclude your meal with Stroganoff Chicken Liver with Mushrooms and Cream. This dish promises a rich and indulgent dining experience. Whether you're exploring new flavors or revisiting traditional favorites, this recipe from our Slow Cooker Cookbook offers a deliciously unique way to enjoy the classic stroganoff, making it a memorable meal for any occasion.

Recipe 10: Chicken and Dumplings

Embrace the comfort of home-cooked meals with "Casserole Dish of Chicken and Dumplings," a heartwarming recipe from our Slow Cooker Cookbook. This dish combines tender chicken, fluffy dumplings, and a creamy sauce in a symphony of flavors and textures epitomizing comfort food. It's a satisfying meal that feels like a warm hug, perfect for those chilly evenings or whenever you crave a touch of nostalgia.

Servings: 2   **Cook Time:** 6 hours

Prepping Time: 20 minutes   **Difficulty:** Easy

Ingredients:

- ✓ 2 chicken breasts, cut into pieces
- ✓ 1 can (10.5 oz) cream of chicken soup
- ✓ 1 cup chicken broth
- ✓ 1 onion, diced
- ✓ 1 cup all-purpose flour
- ✓ 2 teaspoons baking powder
- ✓ 1/2 cup milk
- ✓ Salt and pepper to taste
- ✓ Fresh parsley, chopped, for garnish

Step-by-Step Preparation:

1. Place chicken, cream of chicken soup, chicken broth, and onion in the slow cooker. Season with salt and pepper.
2. Cook on low for 5 hours until chicken is tender.
3. Mix flour, baking powder, and milk to form a soft dough for the dumplings.
4. Drop spoonfuls of dumpling dough into the slow cooker.
5. Cook on high for an additional hour until dumplings are cooked through.
6. Garnish with fresh parsley before serving.

Nutritional Facts: (Per serving)

- ❖ Calories: 550
- ❖ Protein: 55g
- ❖ Carbohydrates: 55g
- ❖ Fat: 15g
- ❖ Sodium: 950mg
- ❖ Fiber: 3g

Conclude your meal with a Casserole Dish of Chicken and Dumplings, a dish that feeds the body and comforts the soul. Whether you're gathering around the table with family or enjoying a quiet meal, this recipe from our Slow Cooker Cookbook provides a simple yet profoundly satisfying way to enjoy the timeless appeal of chicken and dumplings.

CHAPTER 04: VEGGIE ROMANCE

Recipe 01: Ratatouille

Embark on a culinary journey to the heart of Provence with "Ratatouille with Vegetables," a vibrant dish from our Slow Cooker Cookbook. This quintessentially French recipe celebrates the simplicity and elegance of summer vegetables, slow-cooked to perfection, creating a symphony of flavors and textures. Ideal for those seeking a healthy and colorful meal, it's a testament to the beauty of vegetables when cooked with care and passion.

Servings: 2

Cook Time: 6 hours

Prepping Time: 20 minutes

Difficulty: Easy

Ingredients:

- ✓ 1 eggplant, cubed
- ✓ 2 zucchinis, sliced
- ✓ 1 bell pepper, chopped
- ✓ 2 tomatoes, diced
- ✓ 1 onion, chopped
- ✓ 2 cloves garlic, minced
- ✓ 2 tablespoons olive oil
- ✓ 1 teaspoon dried thyme
- ✓ Salt and pepper to taste

Step-by-Step Preparation:

1. Combine all vegetables in the slow cooker.
2. Add garlic, olive oil, thyme, salt, and pepper.
3. Stir to ensure vegetables are evenly coated with seasonings.
4. Cook on low for 6 hours, until vegetables are tender and flavors meld.
5. Adjust seasoning if necessary before serving.

Nutritional Facts: (Per serving)

- ❖ Calories: 200
- ❖ Protein: 5g
- ❖ Carbohydrates: 30g
- ❖ Fat: 10g
- ❖ Sodium: 30mg
- ❖ Fiber: 9g

Conclude your meal with Ratatouille with Vegetables, a dish that embodies the essence of French country cooking. Whether enjoyed as a main course or a side dish, this recipe from our Slow Cooker Cookbook offers a delightful way to savor the garden's bounty, bringing a piece of Provencal sunshine to your table.

Recipe 02: Mushrooms Curry

Discover the rich and aromatic world of "Mushrooms Curry with Creamy Sauce," a luxurious dish from our Slow Cooker Cookbook. This vegetarian delight combines earthy mushrooms with a decadent, spiced, creamy sauce, offering a perfect blend of flavors. Ideal for those seeking a gourmet meatless option, it's a testament to how vegetarian dishes can be just as indulgent and satisfying as their meat-based counterparts.

Servings: 2

Cook Time: 6 hours

Prepping Time: 15 minutes

Difficulty: Easy

Ingredients:

- ✓ 2 cups mushrooms, sliced
- ✓ 1 onion, finely chopped
- ✓ 2 cloves garlic, minced
- ✓ 1 cup coconut milk
- ✓ 2 teaspoons curry powder
- ✓ 1 teaspoon garam masala
- ✓ Salt and pepper to taste
- ✓ Fresh cilantro for garnish
- ✓ 1 tablespoon olive oil

Step-by-Step Preparation:

1. Sauté onion and garlic in olive oil until soft. Transfer to the slow cooker.
2. Add mushrooms, coconut milk, curry powder, garam masala, salt, and pepper to the slow cooker.
3. Stir well to combine all the ingredients.
4. Cook on low for 6 hours, allowing the flavors to meld and the sauce to thicken.
5. Garnish with fresh cilantro before serving.

Nutritional Facts: (Per serving)

- ❖ Calories: 300
- ❖ Protein: 5g
- ❖ Carbohydrates: 15g
- ❖ Fat: 25g
- ❖ Sodium: 200mg
- ❖ Fiber: 3g

Conclude your meal with Mushrooms Curry with Creamy Sauce, a dish that promises a delightful exploration of flavors and textures. Whether you're a vegetarian or simply looking to incorporate more plant-based meals into your diet, this recipe from our Slow Cooker Cookbook offers a delicious and easy way to enjoy the complex flavors of curry in a comforting, creamy sauce.

Recipe 03: Casserole With Sweet Potato

Immerse yourself in the hearty and nourishing flavors of "Casserole with Sweet Potato, Kale, and Sausage," a comforting dish from our Slow Cooker Cookbook. This recipe skillfully combines the sweetness of sweet potatoes with the earthiness of kale and the savory richness of sausage. Perfect for those seeking a warm, satisfying meal, it's a wholesome choice that delivers taste and nutrition.

Servings: 2

Cook Time: 6 hours

Prepping Time: 15 minutes

Difficulty: Easy

Ingredients:

- ✓ 2 sweet potatoes, peeled and cubed
- ✓ 2 cups kale, chopped
- ✓ 1/2 lb sausage, sliced
- ✓ 1 onion, chopped
- ✓ 2 cloves garlic, minced
- ✓ 1 cup chicken broth
- ✓ Salt and pepper to taste
- ✓ 1 teaspoon smoked paprika

Step-by-Step Preparation:

1. Layer sweet potatoes, kale, sausage, onion, and garlic in the slow cooker.
2. Season with salt, pepper, and smoked paprika.
3. Pour chicken broth over the mixture.
4. Cook on low for 6 hours until sweet potatoes are tender, and flavors are well combined.
5. Stir gently before serving to mix all the ingredients.

Nutritional Facts: (Per serving)

- ❖ Calories: 450
- ❖ Protein: 15g
- ❖ Carbohydrates: 50g
- ❖ Fat: 20g
- ❖ Sodium: 800mg
- ❖ Fiber: 7g

Conclude your meal with Casserole with Sweet Potato, Kale, and Sausage, a dish that celebrates the comfort of slow-cooked meals. Whether you need a cozy dinner on a cold night or a nutritious meal any day, this recipe from our Slow Cooker Cookbook offers a delightful way to enjoy the hearty goodness of simple yet flavorful ingredients.

Recipe 04: Cauliflower Cheese

Savor the creamy and comforting "Cauliflower Cheese in a Baking Form," a classic dish reimagined from our Slow Cooker Cookbook. This recipe transforms cauliflower into a sumptuous feast with velvety cheese sauce, baked to golden perfection. Ideal for those seeking a comforting vegetarian option or a delightful side dish, it's a simple yet indulgent way to enjoy the wholesome goodness of cauliflower.

Servings: 2

Prepping Time: 15 minutes

Cook Time: 2.5 hours

Difficulty: Easy

Ingredients:

- ✓ 1 head cauliflower, cut into florets
- ✓ 1 cup cheddar cheese, grated
- ✓ 1/2 cup milk
- ✓ 2 tablespoons flour
- ✓ 2 tablespoons butter
- ✓ Salt and pepper to taste
- ✓ Nutmeg, a pinch

Step-by-Step Preparation:

1. Steam cauliflower florets until just tender. Place in a baking form.
2. In a saucepan, melt butter, whisk in flour, and gradually add milk to make a roux.
3. Add grated cheese to the roux, stirring until smooth. Season with salt, pepper, and nutmeg.
4. Pour the cheese sauce over the cauliflower in the baking form.
5. Bake in a slow cooker set to high or in an oven at 375°F for 25 minutes until golden.
6. Serve warm, enjoying the creamy texture and rich flavor.

Nutritional Facts: (Per serving)

- ❖ Calories: 380
- ❖ Protein: 18g
- ❖ Carbohydrates: 18g
- ❖ Fat: 26g
- ❖ Sodium: 500mg
- ❖ Fiber: 3g

Conclude your meal with Cauliflower Cheese in a Baking Form. This dish promises a heartwarming blend of flavors and textures. Whether as a main for vegetarians or a side for a larger meal, this recipe from our Slow Cooker Cookbook delivers a comforting and satisfying experience, showcasing how simple ingredients can be transformed into a deliciously rich and creamy dish.

Recipe 05: Brinjal Curry

Explore the depths of flavor with "Brinjal Curry," an irresistible recipe from our Slow Cooker Cookbook. This dish centers around brinjal, or eggplant, simmered in a rich, spicy curry sauce that melds the complex flavors of traditional spices. Perfect for those who appreciate the robust tastes of South Asian cuisine, it's a vegetarian delight that promises to be a comforting and aromatic meal.

Servings: 2

Cook Time: 6 hours

Prepping Time: 15 minutes

Difficulty: Easy

Ingredients:

- ✓ 2 large brinjals (eggplants), cubed
- ✓ 1 onion, finely chopped
- ✓ 2 tomatoes, diced
- ✓ 2 cloves garlic, minced
- ✓ 1 teaspoon ground turmeric
- ✓ 1 teaspoon ground cumin
- ✓ 1 teaspoon ground coriander
- ✓ 1/2 teaspoon chili powder
- ✓ 1 cup coconut milk
- ✓ Salt to taste
- ✓ Fresh cilantro for garnish

Step-by-Step Preparation:

1. Place the cubed brinjals, onion, tomatoes, and garlic in the slow cooker.
2. Add turmeric, cumin, coriander, chili powder, and salt.
3. Pour in coconut milk and stir to combine all ingredients.
4. Cook on low for 6 hours, until brinjals are tender and the sauce is thick.
5. Garnish with fresh cilantro before serving.

Nutritional Facts: (Per serving)

- ❖ Calories: 250
- ❖ Protein: 5g
- ❖ Carbohydrates: 20g
- ❖ Fat: 18g
- ❖ Sodium: 300mg
- ❖ Fiber: 7g

Conclude your meal with Brinjal Curry, which brings flavor and warmth to any dining table. Whether served with rice or bread, this recipe from our Slow Cooker Cookbook offers a delightful way to enjoy eggplant, transforming it with spices and coconut milk into a rich, comforting curry that's both nourishing and satisfying.

Recipe 06: Vegan Spinach Artichoke

Dive into the creamy and indulgent world of "Vegan Spinach Artichoke Dip," a delightful recipe from our Slow Cooker Cookbook, perfect for sharing. This dip reimagines the classic favorite with a vegan twist, combining tender spinach and artichokes in a rich, savory sauce, served with crispy pita for dipping. It's designed for those seeking a plant-based option without compromising taste or texture, making it an ideal choice for any gathering.

Servings: 2

Cook Time: 2 hours

Prepping Time: 15 minutes

Difficulty: Easy

Ingredients:

- ✓ 1 cup canned artichoke hearts, drained and chopped
- ✓ 2 cups fresh spinach, chopped
- ✓ 1 cup unsweetened almond milk
- ✓ 1 cup cashews, soaked and drained
- ✓ 2 cloves garlic, minced
- ✓ 1 tablespoon nutritional yeast
- ✓ Salt and pepper to taste
- ✓ Pita bread for serving

Step-by-Step Preparation:

1. Blend cashews, almond milk, garlic, and nutritional yeast until smooth.
2. Combine the cashew mixture with chopped artichokes and spinach in the slow cooker.
3. Season with salt and pepper, stirring to combine.
4. Cook on low for 2 hours, until the dip is hot and flavors have melded.
5. Serve with pita bread for dipping.

Nutritional Facts: (Per serving)

- ❖ Calories: 350
- ❖ Protein: 12g
- ❖ Carbohydrates: 40g
- ❖ Fat: 18g
- ❖ Sodium: 300mg
- ❖ Fiber: 6g

Conclude your meal or start your party with a Vegan Spinach Artichoke Dip, which brings everyone together. Whether it's a casual get-together or a formal feast, this recipe from our Slow Cooker Cookbook offers a delectable way to enjoy a beloved classic, ensuring a guilt-free and satisfying experience for vegans and non-vegans alike.

Recipe 07: Garlic Potatoes

Discover the bold flavors of "Lebanese Garlic Potatoes with Cilantro," a vibrant dish from our Slow Cooker Cookbook that brings the essence of Lebanese cuisine to your table. This recipe features perfectly cooked potatoes infused with garlic sauce and a generous amount of fresh cilantro, offering a delightful combination of textures and tastes. It's ideal for those who appreciate the aromatic and hearty side of Mediterranean cooking, making it a perfect complement to any meal.

Servings: 2

Prepping Time: 15 minutes

Cook Time: 3 hours

Difficulty: Easy

Ingredients:

- ✓ 4 large potatoes, cubed
- ✓ 4 cloves garlic, minced
- ✓ 1/2 cup fresh cilantro, chopped
- ✓ 3 tablespoons olive oil
- ✓ Salt and pepper to taste
- ✓ 1 lemon, juiced

Step-by-Step Preparation:

1. Place the cubed potatoes in the slow cooker.
2. Mix olive oil, garlic, cilantro, salt, and pepper in a small bowl.
3. Pour the mixture over the potatoes and stir to ensure even coating.
4. Cook on high for 3 hours until potatoes are tender.
5. Drizzle with lemon juice before serving.

Nutritional Facts: (Per serving)

- ❖ Calories: 300
- ❖ Protein: 5g
- ❖ Carbohydrates: 45g
- ❖ Fat: 12g
- ❖ Sodium: 200mg
- ❖ Fiber: 6g

Conclude your dining experience with Lebanese Garlic Potatoes with Cilantro. This dish promises a burst of flavor in every bite. Whether part of a feast or a simple meal, this recipe from our Slow Cooker Cookbook provides a delicious way to enjoy the simplicity of potatoes, elevated by the robust flavors of garlic and cilantro, for a truly memorable dish.

Recipe 08: Spinach Potatoes Curry

Embark on a flavorful voyage with "Spinach Potatoes Curry," a nourishing and vibrant dish from our Slow Cooker Cookbook. This recipe combines the earthy comfort of potatoes with the fresh, green goodness of spinach, all simmered in a richly spiced curry sauce. Ideal for those seeking a hearty, plant-based meal, it's a delightful way to enjoy the fusion of simple ingredients and complex flavors.

Servings: 2

Cook Time: 6 hours

Prepping Time: 20 minutes

Difficulty: Easy

Ingredients:

- ✓ 2 large potatoes, cubed
- ✓ 2 cups spinach, chopped
- ✓ 1 onion, chopped
- ✓ 2 cloves garlic, minced
- ✓ 1 can (14 oz) coconut milk
- ✓ 1 tablespoon curry powder
- ✓ 1 teaspoon ground turmeric
- ✓ Salt and pepper to taste
- ✓ Fresh cilantro for garnish

Step-by-Step Preparation:

1. Place potatoes, spinach, onion, and garlic in the slow cooker.
2. In a bowl, mix coconut milk, curry powder, and turmeric.
3. Pour the coconut milk mixture over the vegetables in the slow cooker.
4. Season with salt and pepper.
5. Cook on low for 6 hours until potatoes are tender and flavors have melded.
6. Garnish with fresh cilantro before serving.

Nutritional Facts: (Per serving)

- ❖ Calories: 350
- ❖ Protein: 6g
- ❖ Carbohydrates: 50g
- ❖ Fat: 14g
- ❖ Sodium: 200mg
- ❖ Fiber: 8g

Conclude your meal with Spinach Potatoes Curry, a dish that brings a comforting and satisfying experience. Whether it's a chilly evening or you're simply in the mood for a flavorful curry, this recipe from our Slow Cooker Cookbook offers a beautiful way to enjoy the wholesome combination of spinach and potatoes, enhanced by the warm embrace of curry spices.

Recipe 09: Casserole Dish of Spinach

Indulge in the luxurious simplicity of "Casserole Dish of Spinach in Cream Sauce," a decadent creation from our Slow Cooker Cookbook. This dish elevates the humble spinach to gourmet levels, bathing it in a rich, velvety cream sauce. Perfect for those seeking a side dish that combines comfort with a touch of elegance, it's a testament to how a few quality ingredients can transform into something extraordinary.

Servings: 2

Cook Time: 2 hours

Prepping Time: 10 minutes

Difficulty: Easy

Ingredients:

- ✓ 2 cups fresh spinach
- ✓ 1 cup heavy cream
- ✓ 2 cloves garlic, minced
- ✓ 1/2 onion, finely chopped
- ✓ 1/4 cup grated Parmesan cheese
- ✓ Salt and pepper to taste
- ✓ Nutmeg, a pinch

Step-by-Step Preparation:

1. Place spinach, garlic, and onion in the slow cooker.
2. Pour heavy cream over the spinach mixture.
3. Season with salt, pepper, and a pinch of nutmeg.
4. Cook on low for 2 hours, until the spinach is tender and the sauce thickens.
5. Stir in grated Parmesan cheese until melted and combined.
6. Serve the spinach in cream sauce hot as a luxurious side.

Nutritional Facts: (Per serving)

- ❖ Calories: 400
- ❖ Protein: 8g
- ❖ Carbohydrates: 8g
- ❖ Fat: 38g
- ❖ Sodium: 300mg
- ❖ Fiber: 1g

Conclude your meal with a Casserole Dish of Spinach in Cream Sauce, a dish that promises a creamy and comforting delight. Whether accompanying a main course or enjoyed on its own, this recipe from our Slow Cooker Cookbook offers a rich and flavorful way to savor spinach, showcasing the vegetable's versatility and the indulgent appeal of cream sauce.

Recipe 10: Vegetable Ragout

Immerse yourself in the rustic charm of "Vegetable Ragout," a heartwarming recipe from our Slow Cooker Cookbook. This dish is a celebration of vegetables, slow-cooked in a rich and savory broth that enhances their natural flavors. Perfect for those seeking a comforting and nutritious meal, it's a versatile dish that showcases the beauty and depth of seasonal produce, making it a delightful choice for any occasion.

Servings: 2

Cook Time: 6 hours

Prepping Time: 20 minutes

Difficulty: Easy

Ingredients:

- ✓ 1 carrot, chopped
- ✓ 1 zucchini, chopped
- ✓ 1 bell pepper, chopped
- ✓ 1 onion, chopped
- ✓ 2 tomatoes, diced
- ✓ 1 cup vegetable broth
- ✓ 1 teaspoon dried basil
- ✓ 1 teaspoon dried oregano
- ✓ Salt and pepper to taste

Step-by-Step Preparation:

1. Place all chopped vegetables in the slow cooker.
2. Add diced tomatoes and vegetable broth.
3. Season with basil, oregano, salt, and pepper.
4. Stir to combine all ingredients well.
5. Cook on low for 6 hours, until vegetables are tender and flavors meld together.
6. Adjust seasoning if necessary before serving.

Nutritional Facts: (Per serving)

- ❖ Calories: 150
- ❖ Protein: 4g
- ❖ Carbohydrates: 30g
- ❖ Fat: 1g
- ❖ Sodium: 300mg
- ❖ Fiber: 8g

Conclude your meal with Vegetable Ragout, a dish that nourishes the body and warms the soul. Whether enjoyed as a main or a side, this recipe from our Slow Cooker Cookbook offers a simple yet satisfying way to savor the garden's bounty, bringing together a medley of vegetables in a flavorful and comforting stew.

CHAPTER 05: SOOTHING SOUPS

Recipe 01: Spanish Tomato

Embark on a culinary journey to the heart of Spain with "Spanish Tomato Soup," a vibrant dish from our Slow Cooker Cookbook. This recipe captures the essence of Spanish cuisine, combining ripe tomatoes, garlic, and a blend of spices to create a soup that's both comforting and bursting with flavor. It's ideal for a light lunch or a flavorful starter, perfect for those who love bold Mediterranean flavors.

Servings: 2

Prepping Time: 15 minutes

Cook Time: 4 hours

Difficulty: Easy

Ingredients:

- ✓ 4 large tomatoes, diced
- ✓ 1 onion, chopped
- ✓ 2 cloves garlic, minced
- ✓ 2 cups vegetable broth
- ✓ 1 teaspoon smoked paprika
- ✓ 1/2 teaspoon cumin
- ✓ Salt and pepper to taste
- ✓ Fresh basil for garnish
- ✓ Croutons, for serving

Step-by-Step Preparation:

1. Place tomatoes, onion, and garlic in the slow cooker.
2. Add vegetable broth, smoked paprika, and cumin. Season with salt and pepper.
3. Cook on low for 4 hours, until the tomatoes are soft and the flavors have melded.
4. Blend the soup until smooth.
5. Serve hot, garnished with fresh basil, and accompanied by croutons.

Nutritional Facts: (Per serving)

- ❖ Calories: 90
- ❖ Protein: 3g
- ❖ Carbohydrates: 20g
- ❖ Fat: 1g
- ❖ Sodium: 300mg
- ❖ Fiber: 5g

Conclude your meal with Spanish Tomato Soup, a dish that offers a taste of Spain's rich culinary heritage. Whether it's a fantastic evening or you're simply in the mood for a flavorful soup, this recipe from our Slow Cooker Cookbook delivers a delicious and easy way to enjoy the classic combination of tomatoes and spices, making every spoonful a delightful experience.

Recipe 02: Chicken Vegetable Noodle

Warm up with "Chicken Noodle and Vegetable Soup," a comforting classic from our Slow Cooker Cookbook. This wholesome dish combines tender chicken, nourishing vegetables, and hearty noodles in a flavorful broth, making it perfect for those chilly days or when needing a comforting meal. Ideal for health-conscious individuals looking for a satisfying and easy-to-prepare option, it's a bowl full of goodness that promises to delight and nourish.

Servings: 2

Prepping Time: 20 minutes

Cook Time: 6 hours

Difficulty: Easy

Ingredients:

- ✓ 2 chicken breasts, cubed
- ✓ 1 cup carrots, sliced
- ✓ 1 cup celery, sliced
- ✓ 1 onion, chopped
- ✓ 2 cloves garlic, minced
- ✓ 4 cups chicken broth
- ✓ 1 cup egg noodles
- ✓ 1 teaspoon dried thyme
- ✓ Salt and pepper to taste
- ✓ Fresh parsley, chopped, for garnish

Step-by-Step Preparation:

1. Place chicken, carrots, celery, onion, and garlic in the slow cooker.
2. Pour chicken broth over the ingredients and season with thyme, salt, and pepper.
3. Cook on low for 6 hours, until chicken is tender and vegetables are soft.
4. Add egg noodles during the last 30 minutes of cooking.
5. Serve hot, garnished with fresh parsley.

Nutritional Facts: (Per serving)

- ❖ Calories: 300
- ❖ Protein: 25g
- ❖ Carbohydrates: 30g
- ❖ Fat: 10g
- ❖ Sodium: 700mg
- ❖ Fiber: 3g

Conclude your meal with Chicken Noodle and Vegetable Soup, a dish that brings comfort and nutrition to the forefront. Whether you're seeking solace in a bowl during the winter months or looking for a light yet fulfilling meal, this recipe from our Slow Cooker Cookbook offers a delightful way to enjoy timeless flavors in a healthy, satisfying manner.

Recipe 03: Mushroom Barley

Savor the earthy flavors of "Mushroom Barley Soup," a hearty and wholesome dish from our Slow Cooker Cookbook. This soup combines the rich, umami taste of mushrooms with the chewy texture of barley, creating a comforting bowl that's both nourishing and satisfying. Ideal for those seeking a warm, rustic meal, it's a perfect choice for a cozy night in or a nutritious lunch option.

Servings: 2

Prepping Time: 15 minutes

Cook Time: 6 hours

Difficulty: Easy

Ingredients:

- ✓ 1 cup mushrooms, sliced
- ✓ 1/2 cup pearl barley
- ✓ 1 onion, chopped
- ✓ 2 cloves garlic, minced
- ✓ 4 cups vegetable broth
- ✓ 1 carrot, diced
- ✓ 1 celery stalk, diced
- ✓ 1 teaspoon thyme
- ✓ Salt and pepper to taste
- ✓ Fresh parsley for garnish

Step-by-Step Preparation:

1. Place mushrooms, barley, onion, garlic, carrot, and celery in the slow cooker.
2. Pour vegetable broth over the mixture.
3. Season with thyme, salt, and pepper.
4. Cook on low for 6 hours until barley is tender and flavors have melded.
5. Serve hot, garnished with fresh parsley.

Nutritional Facts: (Per serving)

- ❖ Calories: 220
- ❖ Protein: 8g
- ❖ Carbohydrates: 45g
- ❖ Fat: 2g
- ❖ Sodium: 600mg
- ❖ Fiber: 10g

Conclude your meal with Mushroom Barley Soup, a dish that not only comforts but also offers a bounty of flavors and textures. Whether you're a mushroom lover or simply searching for a filling, plant-based meal, this recipe from our Slow Cooker Cookbook delivers a delightful experience, proving that simple ingredients can create the most memorable dishes.

Recipe 04: Seafood Chowder

Dive into the creamy depths of "Seafood Chowder," a rich and comforting dish from our Slow Cooker Cookbook. This chowder is a treasure trove of the sea's bounty, combining a variety of seafood with potatoes and corn in a luscious, creamy broth. Perfect for seafood lovers and those seeking warmth on a cold day, it's a bowl of coziness that promises satisfaction with every spoonful.

Servings: 2

Cook Time: 4 hours

Prepping Time: 20 minutes

Difficulty: Medium

Ingredients:

- ✓ 1/2 lb mixed seafood (shrimp, scallops, and clams)
- ✓ 2 potatoes, diced
- ✓ 1 cup corn kernels
- ✓ 1 onion, chopped
- ✓ 2 cloves garlic, minced
- ✓ 2 cups fish or vegetable broth
- ✓ 1 cup heavy cream
- ✓ 1 teaspoon thyme
- ✓ Salt and pepper to taste
- ✓ Fresh parsley for garnish

Step-by-Step Preparation:

1. Place seafood, potatoes, corn, onion, and garlic in the slow cooker.
2. Pour broth over the ingredients, then season with thyme, salt, and pepper.
3. Cook on low for 4 hours, until seafood is cooked and potatoes are tender.
4. Stir in heavy cream during the last 30 minutes of cooking.
5. Serve hot, garnished with fresh parsley.

Nutritional Facts: (Per serving)

- ❖ Calories: 500
- ❖ Protein: 25g
- ❖ Carbohydrates: 40g
- ❖ Fat: 28g
- ❖ Sodium: 700mg
- ❖ Fiber: 5g

Conclude your dining experience with Seafood Chowder, a dish that brings the essence of the ocean to your table. Whether it's a special occasion or a comforting meal you seek, this recipe from our Slow Cooker Cookbook offers a delightful way to enjoy the flavors of the sea, making it a memorable and heartwarming choice for any seafood enthusiast.

Recipe 05: Butternut Squash Apples

Embark on a flavorful journey with "Butternut Squash and Apples Paleo Diet Vegetarian Soup," a harmonious blend from our Slow Cooker Cookbook. This soup marries the sweetness of butternut squash with the tartness of apples, creating a comforting, paleo-friendly meal. Ideal for those on a vegetarian paleo diet, it's a testament to the delicious possibilities of combining simple, wholesome ingredients for a nutritious and satisfying experience.

Servings: 2

Prepping Time: 20 minutes

Cook Time: 6 hours

Difficulty: Easy

Ingredients:

- ✓ 1 butternut squash, peeled and cubed
- ✓ 2 apples, peeled and chopped
- ✓ 1 onion, chopped
- ✓ 2 cups vegetable broth
- ✓ 1 teaspoon cinnamon
- ✓ 1/2 teaspoon nutmeg
- ✓ Salt to taste
- ✓ Coconut cream, for garnish

Step-by-Step Preparation:

1. Combine butternut squash, apples, and onion in the slow cooker.
2. Add vegetable broth, cinnamon, nutmeg, and salt.
3. Cook on low for 6 hours until squash is tender.
4. Puree the soup until smooth using an immersion blender.
5. Serve hot, garnished with a swirl of coconut cream.

Nutritional Facts: (Per serving)

- ❖ Calories: 250
- ❖ Protein: 2g
- ❖ Carbohydrates: 60g
- ❖ Fat: 1g
- ❖ Sodium: 500mg
- ❖ Fiber: 9g

Conclude your meal with Butternut Squash and Apples Paleo Diet Vegetarian Soup. This dish encapsulates the warmth and comfort of home-cooked meals. Whether adhering to a paleo diet or simply seeking a healthy and delicious soup, this recipe from our Slow Cooker Cookbook offers a delightful way to enjoy the natural sweetness and richness of seasonal produce.

Recipe 06: Creamy Broccoli Cheese

Dive into the comforting embrace of "Thick Creamy Broccoli Cheese Soup," a delectable highlight from our Slow Cooker Cookbook. This soup combines the earthy flavor of broccoli with a rich, creamy cheese base, creating a luxurious and satisfying dish. Ideal for cheese lovers and those seeking warmth on a fantastic day, it's a gourmet experience that comforts the soul and delights the palate.

Servings: 2

Prepping Time: 15 minutes

Cook Time: 4 hours

Difficulty: Easy

Ingredients:

- ✓ 2 cups broccoli florets
- ✓ 1 onion, chopped
- ✓ 2 cups vegetable broth
- ✓ 1 cup cheddar cheese, grated
- ✓ 1 cup heavy cream
- ✓ 2 tablespoons flour
- ✓ Salt and pepper to taste
- ✓ Nutmeg, a pinch

Step-by-Step Preparation:

1. Place broccoli and onion in the slow cooker.
2. Pour vegetable broth over the vegetables.
3. Cook on low for 4 hours until broccoli is tender.
4. Blend the soup to the desired thickness.
5. Mix flour with heavy cream, then stir into the soup.
6. Add cheddar cheese, stirring until melted and smooth. Season with salt, pepper, and a pinch of nutmeg.
7. Serve hot, enjoying the creamy, cheesy goodness.

Nutritional Facts: (Per serving)

- ❖ Calories: 550
- ❖ Protein: 20g
- ❖ Carbohydrates: 20g
- ❖ Fat: 45g
- ❖ Sodium: 800mg
- ❖ Fiber: 3g

Conclude your dining experience with Thick Creamy Broccoli Cheese Soup. This dish is a testament to the power of simple ingredients to create profound flavors. Whether you need comfort food or a quick, nutritious meal, this recipe from our Slow Cooker Cookbook delivers a fulfilling and heartwarming bowl of soup that's sure to become a cherished favorite.

Recipe 07: Lentil Soup

Immerse yourself in the wholesome goodness of "Lentil Soup," a soul-satisfying recipe from our Slow Cooker Cookbook. This dish blends the hearty, earthy flavors of lentils with a medley of vegetables simmered to perfection. Ideal for those seeking a nutritious and comforting meal, it's a testament to the simplicity of ingredients coming together to create an intensely flavorful and nourishing experience.

Servings: 2   **Cook Time:** 8 hours

Prepping Time: 15 minutes   **Difficulty:** Easy

Ingredients:

- ✓ 1 cup lentils, rinsed
- ✓ 1 carrot, diced
- ✓ 1 celery stalk, diced
- ✓ 1 onion, chopped
- ✓ 2 cloves garlic, minced
- ✓ 4 cups vegetable broth
- ✓ 1 teaspoon ground cumin
- ✓ Salt and pepper to taste
- ✓ Fresh parsley for garnish

Step-by-Step Preparation:

1. Place lentils, carrots, celery, onion, and garlic in the slow cooker.
2. Add vegetable broth and season with cumin, salt, and pepper.
3. Stir to combine all ingredients.
4. Cook on low for 8 hours until lentils are tender and the soup is flavorful.
5. Adjust seasoning if necessary and garnish with fresh parsley before serving.

Nutritional Facts: (Per serving)

- ❖ Calories: 300
- ❖ Protein: 18g
- ❖ Carbohydrates: 54g
- ❖ Fat: 1g
- ❖ Sodium: 500mg
- ❖ Fiber: 15g

Conclude your meal with Lentil Soup, a dish that brings warmth and comfort with every spoonful. Whether it's a chilly evening or you need a nutritious boost, this recipe from our Slow Cooker Cookbook offers a delightful way to enjoy the benefits of lentils, ensuring a satisfying and healthful dining experience.

Recipe 08: Beans Stew With Sausages

Embark on a flavorful journey with "Beans Stew with Sausages, Herbs, and Spices in Tomato Sauce," a robust dish from our Slow Cooker Cookbook. This hearty stew marries the richness of beans with savory sausages and a symphony of herbs and spices; all simmered in a tangy tomato sauce. Perfect for those seeking comfort food with a kick, it's a fulfilling meal that promises to satisfy your cravings and warm your soul.

Servings: 2

Prepping Time: 20 minutes

Cook Time: 8 hours

Difficulty: Easy

Ingredients:

- ✓ 1 cup dried beans, soaked overnight
- ✓ 2 sausages, sliced
- ✓ 1 onion, chopped
- ✓ 2 cloves garlic, minced
- ✓ 1 can (14 oz) tomato sauce
- ✓ 1 teaspoon dried oregano
- ✓ 1 teaspoon dried basil
- ✓ 1/2 teaspoon smoked paprika
- ✓ Salt and pepper to taste
- ✓ Fresh parsley for garnish

Step-by-Step Preparation:

1. Drain and rinse the soaked beans. Place them in the slow cooker.
2. Add sliced sausages, onion, and garlic.
3. Pour tomato sauce over the ingredients and sprinkle with oregano, basil, and smoked paprika.
4. Season with salt and pepper. Stir to combine.
5. Cook on low for 8 hours until beans are tender and flavors are well blended.
6. Garnish with fresh parsley before serving.

Nutritional Facts: (Per serving)

- ❖ Calories: 500
- ❖ Protein: 25g
- ❖ Carbohydrates: 60g
- ❖ Fat: 20g
- ❖ Sodium: 800mg
- ❖ Fiber: 15g

Conclude your dining experience with bean stew with Sausages, Herbs, and Spices in Tomato Sauce. This dish embodies the essence of hearty cooking. Whether it's a casual dinner or a cozy night in, this recipe from our Slow Cooker Cookbook delivers a rich and satisfying stew that's sure to become a cherished addition to your culinary repertoire.

Recipe 09: Thai Shrimp Red Curry

Embark on a culinary adventure with "Thai Chicken Shrimp Red Curry Soup," an irresistible dish from our Slow Cooker Cookbook. This soup blends the juiciness of chicken and shrimp with the exotic flavors of Thai red curry, coconut milk, and various vegetables, creating a spicy, aromatic, and creamy concoction. Ideal for those craving a fusion of flavors, it's a delightful way to experience the warmth and complexity of Thai cuisine.

Servings: 2

Prepping Time: 20 minutes

Cook Time: 4 hours

Difficulty: Medium

Ingredients:

- ✓ 1/2 lb chicken breast, cubed
- ✓ 1/2 lb shrimp, peeled and deveined
- ✓ 2 tablespoons Thai red curry paste
- ✓ 1 can (14 oz) coconut milk
- ✓ 1 cup chicken broth
- ✓ 1 bell pepper, sliced
- ✓ 1 onion, chopped
- ✓ 1 carrot, sliced
- ✓ 1 tablespoon fish sauce
- ✓ 1 teaspoon sugar
- ✓ Fresh basil for garnish
- ✓ Lime wedges for serving

Step-by-Step Preparation:

1. Place chicken, shrimp, bell pepper, onion, and carrot in the slow cooker.
2. Whisk together red curry paste, coconut milk, chicken broth, fish sauce, and sugar in a bowl.
3. Pour the mixture over the ingredients in the slow cooker.
4. Cook on low for 4 hours, until chicken and shrimp are cooked.
5. Serve hot, garnished with fresh basil and lime wedges on the side.

Nutritional Facts: (Per serving)

- ❖ Calories: 450
- ❖ Protein: 35g
- ❖ Carbohydrates: 15g
- ❖ Fat: 30g
- ❖ Sodium: 800mg
- ❖ Fiber: 3g

Conclude your meal with Thai Chicken Shrimp Red Curry Soup. This dish offers a rich tapestry of flavors, from the spicy kick of red curry to the creamy sweetness of coconut milk. Whether you're a seasoned lover of Thai food or exploring new tastes, this recipe from our Slow Cooker Cookbook provides a delicious and authentic experience, perfect for any occasion.

Recipe 10: Chicken Corn

Savor the comforting embrace of "Chicken Corn Soup with Egg," a heartwarming recipe from our Slow Cooker Cookbook. This soup elevates the classic chicken corn combination with the silky richness of a beaten egg, creating a soothing and nutritious dish. Ideal for those seeking a touch of warmth and wholesomeness, it's a beautifully simple yet satisfying meal that promises to nourish and delight with every spoonful.

Servings: 2

Prepping Time: 15 minutes

Cook Time: 6 hours

Difficulty: Easy

Ingredients:

- ✓ 2 chicken breasts
- ✓ 1 cup corn kernels
- ✓ 4 cups chicken broth
- ✓ 1 onion, chopped
- ✓ 2 cloves garlic, minced
- ✓ 1 egg, lightly beaten
- ✓ Salt and pepper to taste
- ✓ Green onions, sliced, for garnish

Step-by-Step Preparation:

1. Place chicken, corn, onion, and garlic in the slow cooker.
2. Pour chicken broth over the ingredients, seasoning with salt and pepper.
3. Cook on low for 6 hours until chicken is tender.
4. Shred the chicken back into the soup.
5. Slowly stir in the beaten egg, creating ribbons in the hot soup.
6. Serve garnished with sliced green onions.

Nutritional Facts: (Per serving)

- ❖ Calories: 230
- ❖ Protein: 32g
- ❖ Carbohydrates: 21g
- ❖ Fat: 4g
- ❖ Sodium: 960mg
- ❖ Fiber: 2g

Conclude your meal with Chicken Corn Soup with Egg, a dish that captures the essence of comforting, homemade soup. Whether you're seeking solace on a cold day or a light yet fulfilling meal, this recipe from our Slow Cooker Cookbook delivers a delightful combination of flavors and textures, making it a timeless classic for any occasion.

Conclusion

In "Delicious Slow Cooker Recipes for Two: Healthy Cooking Ideas With Mouthwatering Images," Clara Levine masterfully guides couples through slow cooking, presenting a collection that simplifies mealtime and elevates it into an intimate culinary adventure. From the tender embrace of seafood entrees to the comforting warmth of hearty stews, each recipe is a testament to the power of slow cooking to transform simple ingredients into exquisite meals that cater perfectly to the tastes and schedules of modern couples.

Imagine coming home to the seductive aroma of a ready-to-serve gourmet meal. This kind promises not just nourishment but an experience. This book brings that vision to life, offering a way to enjoy luxury dining without leaving the comfort of your home. With Clara Levine's expert guidance, you'll unlock the secrets to crafting delectable dishes that are as nutritious as they are flavorful.

Delve into pages filled with stunning images that do more than showcase food; they tell a story of love, companionship, and the joy of sharing a meal. Each recipe is carefully designed for two, ensuring that you waste less while still enjoying a variety of dishes that span global cuisines—from the robust flavors of a classic Italian stew to the subtle aromas of Asian-inspired soups.

Beyond recipes, this book offers a journey into healthier eating, with dishes that utilize fresh, whole ingredients. It's perfect for couples looking to expand their culinary repertoire or anyone seeking to create memorable meals with minimal effort. The slow cooker does the heavy lifting, allowing you to spend less time in the kitchen and more time enjoying the company of your loved one.

"Delicious Slow Cooker Recipes for Two" is more than a cookbook—it's a gateway to creating moments that matter. Available in both Kindle and Paperback formats, it's time to turn the page on your cooking routine. Embrace the ease, the flavor, and the joy of slow cooking. Order your copy today and start a new tradition of togetherness and delicious dining.

End your day on a note of satisfaction and anticipation for the next culinary exploration, knowing that "Delicious Slow Cooker Recipes for Two" is not just a book but a companion in your journey towards a more prosperous, more flavorful life.

Made in the USA
Coppell, TX
22 November 2024

40786883R00059